Baby Owl Lost Her Whoo

Written and Illustrated by
Cindy R. Lee

Cindy R. Lee, LCSW
PO Box 14060
Oklahoma City, OK 73113

The "Who is the Boss?" concept as it relates to "children from hard places" was derived from the Trust-Based Relational Intervention® resources (Purvis & Cross, 1999-2014.) For more information please read Purvis, K.B., Cross, D.R. & Sunshine, W.L. (2007) *The Connected Child: Bringing Hope and Healing to Your Adoptive Family.* New York: McGraw-Hill.

Acknowledgements

Special thanks to Kelly and Amy Gray, David and Jean McLaughlin and the McLaughlin Family Foundation for giving the gift of healing to foster and adopted children. Thank you to Casey Call and Henry Milton for their on-going support and teaching, to Ibis for crocheting baby owls, to Melissa Brunner for reading multiple versions of the book, to Jennifer Abney and Brooke Hayes for ongoing support, to Cheryl Devoe and Mike for editing and to my family for all their love and support.

Thank you to Doodle Bug Design, Inc. for allowing the use of 2007 Bubble Blue Sugar Coated Card Stock and 1548 Lily White Sugar Coated Cardstock to create Baby Owl's icy cold illustration.

For Christopher, Amanda
Jack and Mutte

In memory of Pa Pa

Who is the Boss? – Teaching Tips for Parents

By Cindy R. Lee, LCSW, LADC

Imagine for a moment that you just inherited a Fortune 500 company that designs and manufactures computer software. Not only did you inherit the company, but you were appointed CEO. You start on Monday, 7:00 a.m., sharp. All eyes are on you, and the slightest mistake you make may have grave consequences for the 50,000 people employed by you, as well as for the hungry investors. There is just one problem with such an inheritance - you know NOTHING about running a large computer tech corporation! You are not equipped, educated or experienced to meet the needs of this company. In order for the company to survive, you must hire a boss with experience to show you how to do things.

Although the above example is a little ridiculous, it makes you think of how scared and confused you would be taking on such a huge task for which you are not equipped. Children require a boss because they are not equipped to meet their own needs. As their brains and bodies are developing, they need appropriate nutrients, sleep and sensory input. They need information on how to maneuver in the world, and how to stay safe from danger. It is essential that an attentive, nurturing, and strong adult be in charge.

As a means of survival, foster and/or adopted children have learned to be their own boss, and often the boss of their siblings. Although adoptive and/or foster parents desire to provide care, the child's little brain is often already wired to care for himself in order to survive. This characteristic is not unique to foster and adopted children, but may appear in biological children as well. Humans, by nature, often want what they want when they want it. Self-discipline and self-control are traits that must be taught to children, and, it is hoped, are qualities that have been learned by mature adults.

The Best Bosses Aren't Bossy

Many of us have experienced how it felt to work for an ungrateful boss, or one who was obsessed with control. We likely reacted with resentment, and felt that our authentic selves had been suppressed. Creativity, enthusiasm, and hard work were replaced with low motivation and withdrawal. Parenting is similar. You are the boss, and your child needs to know you are the boss, but you should be respectful and not obsessed with control. After all, parenting is about loving, and there is no control or disrespect in unconditional love. The best bosses exercise power when it is needed and share power as much as possible.

How to Share Power

There are three ways to share power: give choices, allow compromises, and say "yes" more often. Children experience a sense of control when they are offered choices. They are given power because they get to choose between two options, and you maintain control because you choose which options to give. For example, if you are trying to get your child to wear cold weather clothing, you can say "Would you like to wear the blue sweater or the gray sweatshirt?"

A compromise happens when the child uses his words to make a deal with you. For example, if you would like for your child to start his homework but he is watching TV, he could ask for a compromise by saying "Mom, May I please finish this show and then start my homework?" You retain power by agreeing or disagreeing to the compromise and the child feels empowered because he is negotiating.

Saying "yes" more often is another way of sharing power with your child. When we frequently say "yes," the child is more likely to accept "no" when it really matters.

The Who is the Boss concept as is relates to parenting "children from hard places" was derived from the Trust-Based Relational Intervention® resources (Purvis & Cross, 1999-2014.) Purvis, K.B., Cross, D.R. & Sunshine, W.L. (2007) *The Connected Child: Bringing Hope and Healing to Your Adoptive Family.* New York: McGraw-Hill.

Who is the Boss? – Teaching Tips for Parents

By Cindy R. Lee, LCSW, LADC

Teaching Your Child the Who's the Boss Concept

Teaching your child this principle starts with an explanation and is then reinforced with games and real life practice.

Parental Explanation:

Avoid lecturing when explaining "Who's the Boss" to your child. The conversation is made fun by reading "Baby Owl Lost Her Whoo," and then discussing the book.

Here is a script you can use as a guide to give a general explanation:

One way mommies and daddies show love is by being the boss. It is hard to have a boss, because we want what we want when we want it. But children need help knowing what to do to stay safe. Mommies and daddies are the boss because they love their children. They want to help them and take care of them. Children don't have to worry about trying to control things because mommy and daddy are the boss. When you don't have to worry about taking care of everything, you can concentrate on playing and having fun.

After reading the book, you can discuss these questions with your child:

- What are some reasons Baby Owl needed a boss?
- If Mommy Owl helps Baby Owl get enough sleep, eat healthy food and wear the right clothes, then what does Baby Owl have time to do? (Answer: play, play, play)
- Who is the boss of you?

Game Participation:

Playing games is a great way to teach new skills and ideas as well. Military Cadence Call (With a Tag Twist) is a fun game you can play with your children.

Military Cadence Call (With a Tag Twist)

Have your children line up in a single file line behind you. Lead your children in a march around your house while chanting this fun military style cadence call. When you get to the last verse, have the children run away from you as you try to tag them.

Left, Left, Left Right Left
Left, Left, Left Right Left
Momma's the boss, oh yes she is.
She shares power; gives choices

Left, Left, Left Right Left
Left, Left, Left Right Left
Daddy's the boss. You bet he is.
He gives us lots of compromises.

Left, Left, Left Right Left
Left, Left, Left Right Left
The game of tag is oh so fun,
I am "it" so you better run!

You can vary the game by calling out different children's names to be "it." Giggles and smiles required.

Real Life Implementation:

Once you have taught the skill, you can use the phrase, "Who's the Boss," in real life situations. For example, if your child wants to pick her dinner, and you need her to eat the dinner you have already prepared, you can say "Mommy is the boss and I need you to eat the dinner I have already prepared." You will not need to offer an explanation because your child has already accepted that you are the boss.

For more books, games and activities, please visit www.cindyrlee.com. For parenting DVD's, visit www.child.tcu.edu. Reading The Connected Child by Dr. Karyn Purvis, Dr. David Cross and Wendi Lyons Sunshine is a must!

The Who is the Boss concept as is relates to parenting "children from hard places" was derived from the Trust-Based Relational Intervention® resources (Purvis & Cross, 1999-2014.) Purvis, K.B., Cross, D.R. & Sunshine, W.L. (2007) *The Connected Child: Bringing Hope and Healing to Your Adoptive Family.* New York: McGraw-Hill.

**Baby Owl was left alone.
"Whoo will be my boss?" she moaned.**

"Whoo will show me what to wear
when the weather is not fair?"

"Without a coat I'll surely freeze.
Whoo will help me, someone please?"

"I should eat healthy all day long.
Fruits and veggies make me strong."

"All I want is food that's sweet.
Whoo will tell me what to eat?"

"Large crowds aren't safe. I could get lost.
Whoo'll stick together? Whoo'll be my boss?"

"Too young to be on my own.
I need a boss so I'm not alone."

"I like swimming in the sun.
Bath time is also fun."

"I'm not safe if I can't swim.
I need a boss so I don't fall in."

"Whoo will help me brush my beak?
Without my boss my beak gets weak."

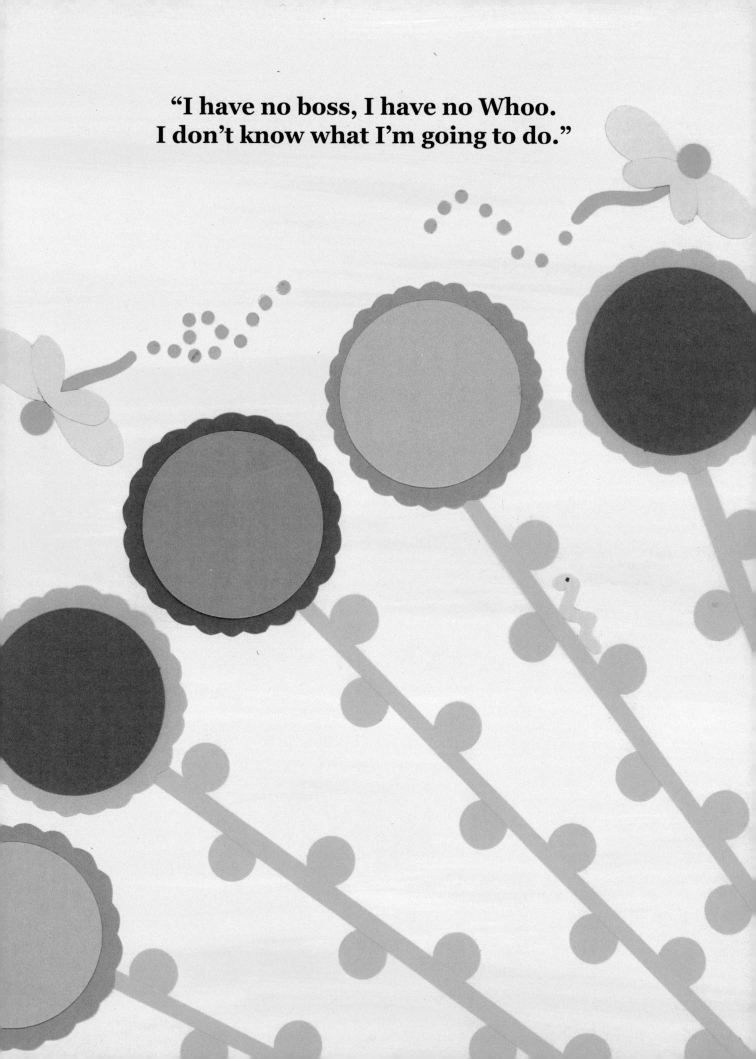

"I have no boss, I have no Whoo.
I don't know what I'm going to do."

"I need sleep to feel just right.
Whoo will tuck me in at night?"

"Without a boss I stay up late.
I may stay up way past eight."

"In the quiet I heard a Whoo.
It was soft and kind and new."

I flew up high so I could see
a mother waiting there for me.

She said, "I'm sorry you've lost your Whoo.
I will show you what to do."

I hugged my mom and kissed her too.
She hugged me back, and away we flew.

About the Author:

Cindy R. Lee is a Licensed Clinical Social Worker and Licensed Alcohol and Drug Counselor in private practice in Oklahoma City, Oklahoma. Cindy is the co-founder and Executive Director of HALO Project, which is a ten-week intensive intervention for foster and adopted children and their families. Cindy lives in Edmond, Oklahoma with her husband Christopher and their children, Amanda and Jack. You can contact Cindy via email at cindy@cindyrlee.com.

Baby Owl Lost Her Whoo *is one of eight children's books designed to teach Trust Based Relational Intervention (TBRI) principles. TBRI is a very successful intervention created by Dr. Karyn Purvis and Dr. David Cross at the Institute of Child Development. For more information, visit www.child.tcu.edu.*